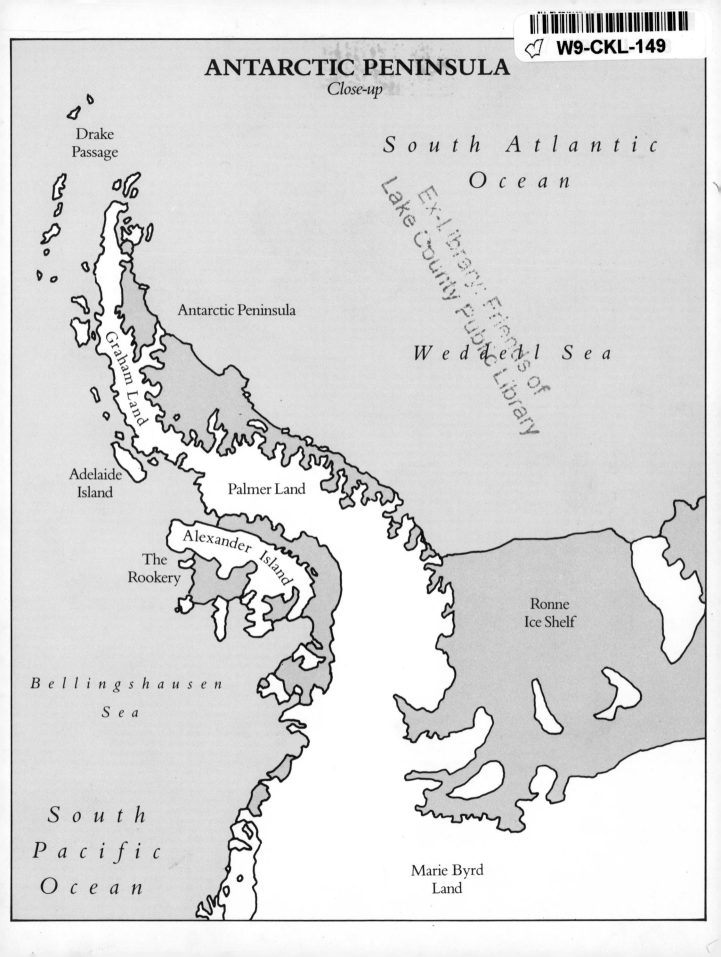

ANTARCTIC PENINSULA
Close-up

Drake
Passage

South Atlantic
Ocean

Antarctic Peninsula

Weddell Sea

Graham Land

Adelaide
Island

Palmer Land

Alexander Island

The
Rookery

Ronne
Ice Shelf

Bellingshausen
Sea

South
Pacific
Ocean

Marie Byrd
Land

Birds of Antarctica

The Adélie Penguin

Jennifer Owings Dewey

Little, Brown and Company

Boston Toronto London

This book is dedicated to

BRINTON C. TURKLE

First edition

Library of Congress Cataloging-in-Publication Data

Dewey, Jennifer Owings
    Birds of Antarctica: The Adélie penguin
    1. Adélie penguin — Juvenile literature. I. Title.
QL696.S473D49   1989   598.4′41   88-13010
ISBN 0-316-18207-9

10 9 8 7 6 5 4 3 2 1

WOR

Published simultaneously in Canada
by Little, Brown & Company (Canada) Limited

Printed in the United States of America

CONTENTS

AUGUST
Summer Begins

In the far north summer is ending;
in the far south it is just beginning.
Snow crystals drift in clouds before the wind,
sweeping and blowing over a vast country, a white land
of snow, ice, and wind shrouded in south polar darkness.
The land is Antarctica, the seventh continent,
the coldest, iciest, windiest place on earth.

Winds scour the ice, shaping it into hills,
valleys, and high plateaus.
Glacial rivers of ice flow slowly toward the coasts.
Mountains traverse the middle of the continent,
jagged black-faced peaks rising nine thousand feet.
Ice near the South Pole is more than two miles thick.
The weight of the ice depresses the land beneath it.

Antarctica's icebound coasts are breeding grounds
for birds migrating out of the north and for Adélie penguins,
birds native to coastal Antarctica.
Antarctica's interior, in the grip of an ice age twenty million
years old, is too cold to support life. The land is barren.
In the southern ocean surrounding Antarctica
and along the edge where ice and rock meet water,
life abounds.

Shambling and scuffling in wavering black-and-white lines,
Adélie penguins cross sea ice ridges, hummocks, and mounds.
The sun is barely above the horizon, its rays casting
shadows on the back sides of ice hills.
Walking in the half-light of an Antarctic spring day,
the Adélies head toward land.
When the sun sinks below the horizon
the Adélies walk on in the dark.
Every day the sun stays up longer.
Every day there is more light.
Sea ice cracks, and pieces crunch against each other.
Bursts of sound like gunshots snap in the frigid air.
These are the only sounds.

Summer is coming, and summer is breeding time for Antarctic birds.
From October to February the sun never goes below the horizon.
Twenty-four hours of daylight give birds time needed
for nesting, mating, egg laying, and raising young.

While the sea ice holds, the Adélie penguins march along,
sometimes flopping on their bellies to scoot faster.
An Adélie sliding on its belly moves twice as fast
as when it walks.
Gradually the sea ice crumbles and cracks.
Sections of it drift with wide, dark seawater leads,
or channels, in between.
The Adélies take to the sea.

SEPTEMBER
Returning from the Sea

Eight Adélie penguins step out of a cold sea onto a stony beach.
Huddling together, the penguins shake water from their
white-feathered breasts and black backs.
All the penguins are males.
Eighteen inches tall, weighing twelve pounds each, the penguins
wag spiky tails and press webbed feet against slippery stones.
The penguins hold up their heads, narrow bills point to the sky.
For a long moment the penguins stay close,
as if deciding what to do.

In one motion the penguins turn and walk up the glistening tide line.
Falling behind each other, single file,
slipping and sliding on wet gravel,
skirting the edge where sea and shore join,
the penguins leave the beach.

Chunks of ice, floes large and small, float on a shiny sea.
The air is cold, sunny, and windless.
Waves lap the shore, rippling and dancing with light.
On the distant horizon, a massive iceberg glows
against a blue sky.

The sea is the Antarctic sea, the southern ocean.
The beach is the shore of an island three miles
off the coast of the Antarctic Peninsula.
The Adélie penguins are returning to their rookery on the island
after seven months at sea.

Leaning into the rocky slope, scraping for footholds, the penguins climb.
Hiking to the top of the island, they reach the highest point.
The rookery, or breeding grounds, covers an acre and a half.
The south-facing rookery is free of snow.

The north side of the island is snow packed.
Cracks and niches in rocks hold pockets of ice.
Water seeps from the bases of moss beds three and four feet thick.
Moss bed surfaces are layered with snow.
Spring thaw is not over.

The penguins break ranks as they enter the rookery.
The male Adélies excitedly search for nests and claim territory.
Each Adélie male knows which nest is his. Females will come later.
Penguins return to the same rookery and the same nest year after year.

Bustling, jostling, colliding, bumping each other,
beating off interference with flippers raised,
penguins cross and recross rough ground.
They croak and jabber as they run.
The island, three miles square, is a hump of fractured,
fissured stone rising out of the sea.
Similar islands in the distance appear as dark spots on blue water.

Scrounging in piles of pebbles, seaweed, and stones,
penguins look for clues.
Each penguin knows when his nest is under him.
When a penguin finds his nest, calls of triumph —
hoots and brays — lift into the cold sky.

Squabbles and fights erupt. All is not peaceful.
Old males battle younger males. With loud, clamorous calls
males three or more years old win all the battles.
These are the males old enough to breed.

Adélie penguins live to be fifteen or twenty years old.
Leopard seals eat them, storms bash them on ice and rock,
some starve to death.
Fights between old and young males, males and females,
or penguins strange to each other go on all the time.
Penguins are argumentative and stubborn.
Nest sites and nest stones are defended with fierce determination.
So are mates.

More Adélies arrive from the beach,
traveling up the same well-worn path
used by generations of penguins.
Newcomers argue over nest sites. They push and elbow and
shove, shouting ringing cries that echo around the rookery.

Rocks, water, and snow are dazzling in the sun.
Noisy penguins arrive in growing numbers.
Meltwater trickles down rock faces
and forms rivers in rock ravines, rock chiseled and sculpted
by centuries of ice and wind. The drip-drip-drip of water
mingles with humming penguin voices.

Females arrive — four days after the males —
and file into the rookery.
They waddle down the path in long lines, their awkward upright
stance on short stumpy legs giving them a rolling walk.
Their short tails trail behind.

The Adélie rookery, now a thousand penguins strong,
becomes a place of chaos and confusion.
Penguins assault each other, quarrel over females, nest sites, and stones.
The ground is overrun with penguin feet and slippery with guano,
littered with pebbles, scattered stones, and seaweed.

Penguins rediscover each other after a winter apart.
Breeding and courting pairs stand stomach to stomach,
toe to toe, heads waggling, beaks skyward, bellowing and
calling and cooing back and forth.
Ear-splitting, boisterous greetings sound out all
over the rookery. Penguins mating for the first time greet
each other with the same displays, the same sounds.
Calls and displays are repeated again and again
during the breeding season.
Once nest sites are chosen, old and new mates claimed,
nest repair and mating begin.

OCTOBER · NOVEMBER
Nesting and Mating

Penguin nests are like shallow bowls, big enough
for a penguin to sit in comfortably.
Made of stones, pebbles, seaweed, and sometimes bones,
nests used over and over have high, mounded sides.
First-time nests are scant rings of stones on the ground.
Both penguin partners work on the nests,
trudging down to the beach, collecting stones and kelp,
carrying everything back in their beaks.

Partner penguins mate often during bouts of nest building.
The male penguin sits on top of the female, balancing
precariously, steadying himself with his flippers and sometimes his bill.
Like other birds, penguins have a single external opening.
The opening is under the tail.
Called a vent, or cloaca, the opening is used
for guano, sperm, and eggs.
Pressing his tail under the female's, the male transfers sperm
from his cloaca to hers.
Sperm travels up a passage called an oviduct.
Reaching the female's eggs, it fertilizes them.
She now can lay fertile eggs.

Round, bluish-white eggs as big as oranges appear in nests
all over the rookery.
One egg is laid and three or four days later a second egg.
Soon almost every penguin pair in the rookery
has eggs to tend and keep warm.
Some penguin pairs will fail to produce any eggs.
They will mate, and no eggs will appear.
They will try again another year.

Other eggs appear in other nests on the island.
Blue-eyed shags and giant petrels brood eggs.
A colony of black-capped terns arrives every year,
settling on the eastern edge of the island.
Terns build nests on inaccessible cliffs.
Like Adélies, terns come in September and October,
the beginning of Antarctica's summer.

Like terns, blue-eyed shags nest in colonies,
often shared with Gentoo penguins.
Gentoos, the same size as Adélies, have bright red bills and red feet.
Shags are cormorants, with long graceful necks and thin hooked beaks.
Cobalt blue eyelids shine brilliantly against black shag faces.
Shag breasts and bellies are white, their backs are black.
In nests of seaweed and sea grass glued with guano,
shags lay four chalk-white eggs.
Shags sit on their eggs, weaving long necks and narrow heads
from side to side, droning and sighing in soft voices.

Brown skuas, predators of Antarctic skies,
pick nest sites close to penguin rookeries.
Skuas prey on penguins.
A skua nest is hardly a nest at all. A sprig of moss,
a fringe of lichen, a depression in the rocks.
Two olive-brown eggs splotched with black,
as big as hen's eggs, are watched and guarded by skua parents.
In solitary pairs, away from other skuas, parents protect their eggs.
Fierce and aggressive aerial attacks drive intruders away.

NOVEMBER · DECEMBER
The Search for Food

Adélie penguins take turns brooding eggs.
Penguin pairs never leave a nest untended.
One penguin is always present.
With nest building, mating, and egg laying finished,
hungry female Adélies leave the rookery and
head for the sea to look for food.

One at a time, then in bands of five or six,
and then in still greater numbers, female Adélies depart.
Troops of females, looking just like males, gather on shore.
Lingering at water's edge, hesitant to plunge in,
females squeeze and crowd together.
Waiting.

Congregated offshore, just under the surface, the sinister
submarine shapes of leopard seals swim up and down.
Leopard seals patrol the seas around the island
in anticipation of penguins diving in.
Sensing danger, penguins put off leaving the beach.
Encounters with leopard seals are fatal.
The seals grab penguins in huge, toothy jaws,
swing them in circles, and strip off their skins.
Leopard seals then eat the soft, fleshy parts.

A full day passes.
Agitated, croaking, hungry penguins reach agreement.
First by dozens, then by hundreds, penguins spill into the sea.
Black-and-white penguin bodies vanish under swirling waves.
Leopard seals will eat a few of them.
But most will survive.

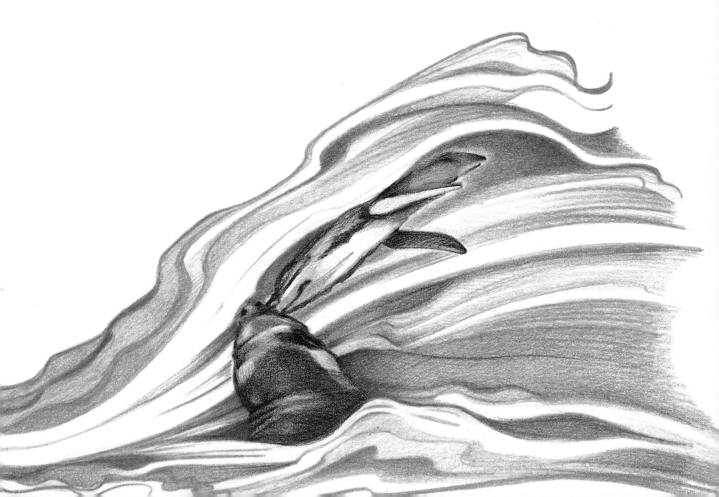

Penguins are clumsy on land.
They sway and roll on stumpy legs,
feet and tail too far back, no waistline, no hips.
Most birds have large wings with flight feathers.
Penguins have narrow, flipper-like wings, useless for flying,
with feathers so small they look like scales.

Swimming penguins "fly" through the water.
Flippers, slender and firm, propel them.
Powerful breast muscles and solid bones give them endurance.
Feet and tail are steering rudders.
Turning sharply in the water, long necks darting left and right,
penguins look for food.
Nearsighted on land, penguins see well under water.
Everything penguins eat is slippery — fish, squid, krill.
Barbs line the penguin's mouth and tongue,
barbs facing backward, down the penguin's throat.
Food is snagged on the barbs.
Swimming at high speeds in the water,
twenty-five or thirty miles an hour,
penguins breathe by leaping into the air
and diving again, never slowing down.

The favored food of penguins is krill.
Pink, soft-shelled, shrimp-like animals with wiggly legs,
krill are as long as a human thumb.
Krill swim toward light, swimming horizontally
near the surface of the sea.
Krill schools, or swarms, are sometimes miles long.

Penguins never drink water.
All the moisture they need is in the food they eat.

Racing through Antarctic seas, leaping for air, and
gulping krill, female penguins travel hundreds of miles
from the island and the rookery.
Their stomachs tell them when to turn and go back.
A stomach filled with krill says "Return" —
and they do.

Krill

DECEMBER · JANUARY
Storm

As the last female Adélie leaves the beach,
a storm tears into the rookery.
Wild winds blow across the island and the sea surrounding it.
With tremendous force, winds carry rain mixed with sleet and with snow.
Visibility in the rookery is reduced to the length of a penguin beak.
Male penguins hunch over nests and eggs, heads down.

Reaching hurricane strength, storm winds toss seas to the sky,
white waves thrashing and enormous.
Winds push drifts of snow against the penguins on their nests
and cover black backs with white coats.
Penguins lift their heads and try to keep bills above the snow.
Winds roar, chafing penguin faces, piling up around
penguin bodies, scouring island beaches,
whistling around corners of rock.

Nesting birds struggle to protect eggs and nests.
With their mates away, feeding in the sea,
male penguins on nests usually take short naps,
snooze and wait for their mates to return.
The storm keeps the penguins alert and alarmed.
The sea surges, waves smash the beaches —
for three days the storm rages.
For three days no penguin stirs from his nest.

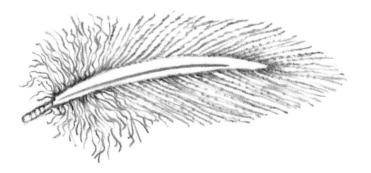

Penguins are warm-blooded and feathered.
Penguins are able to survive Antarctic storms and freezing water.
Their feathers are short, dense, and tightly layered.
Penguins have three hundred feathers to each square inch of skin.
The feathers overlap, like shingles on a roof.
Woolly underdown lies next to the skin.
Beneath the skin, thick blubber is more protection
against bitter cold.

The storm beats itself out.
Miserable, cold, and hungry, all the penguins
in the rookery survive.
Clouds circle the rookery and the island and blow away.
Within a day the winds die, the sun comes out,
the snow turns to slush.
Freezing meltwater pours down the island,
racing in icy rivers through the rookery.
Bright streams cross rocks, rush through nests,
under penguin feet, around nest stones, over eggs.
Some eggs roll away, pulled by the water, left broken,
cracked, and ruined at the bottom of the rookery.
Skuas sweep down on heavy, flapping wings — scoop up
the spilled contents of shattered eggs, fight over the best bits.

A Chick Is Hatched

Fourteen days after leaving the rookery to feed at sea,
the females return.
With stomachs empty, half or a third of their body weight gone,
the brooding males are restless. The brooding urge is strong.
Returning females coax males off eggs,
bumping and nudging them with flippers and bills.
Once pushed completely off the eggs, males greet mates
with bows, flapping flippers, hoots, and trumpeting calls.
Females, bellies full, assume nest duties.

Male Adélies, like females before them,
trundle down the path to the beach.
Bouncing and running, they excitedly head to sea.

Males left mateless stay on their eggs a few days longer.
Near starvation, mateless males are finally driven by hunger
to abandon the eggs and go to sea.
Self-preservation is a powerful force in a penguin brain.

Males left alone will be lucky to find a new mate.
Most will have to wait another year to breed again.

Penguin pairs take turns brooding their eggs,
back and forth, male and female, for thirty-six days in all.
Males sit on the eggs first — for fourteen days.
Females return and brood for a week.
Then males return and brood for another week.
The remaining time is divided into a few days
for each penguin partner.

The Adélie males are usually brooding the eggs in the rookery
when hatching starts.
Sheltered under white breast feathers, warm against a
brood patch, tucked between two penguin feet,
a penguin egg begins hatching when the chick's movement
causes a crack to appear.
A crack as thin as a strand of hair
breaks the waxy smoothness of the shell.

In one hour, maybe two, the crack becomes a hole,
a slot-shaped spot at the end of the egg.
A peeping chick is heard.
Working with spasms of effort the chick jabs,
pokes, pecks, and scratches,
laboring to break the shell around it.
All movement and sound stop when the chick rests.
Beginning again, hammering and peeping, jabbing
its sharp beak at the inner surface of the egg,
the chick struggles to get out.

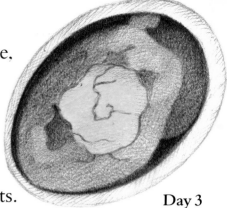

Day 3

Day 9   Day 12   Day 20

Before hatching, a chick inside a penguin egg lies curled
and growing. A watery sac surrounds it.
An air space separates part of the sac from the inside of the shell.
Food comes to the chick through a cord attached to a yolk.
Yolk and cord are connected to a membrane,
a membrane lining the egg.
Blood cells in the membrane draw oxygen
through pores in the shell's surface.
When the chick is ready to hatch, it scratches the sac.
It tears a hole and sticks its head through it.
It reaches the shell and begins pecking at it.
If hatching takes too long the chick
becomes exhausted and dies.

Day before
hatching

New Life in the Rookery

"PEEP! PEEP! PEEP!"
Peeping sounds hang over the rookery like a cloud.
Hundreds of hatching chicks are peeping at once.
Muttering and mumbling parent penguins grunt encouragement.
The peeping of chicks and the calling of parent penguins
is a gentle, soothing noise.
Rushing wings overhead signal the presence of a skua pair.
Skuas are interested in a penguin rookery at hatching time.

First-laid eggs are first to hatch.
Those laid three or four days later hatch
within twenty-four hours of the first ones.
It seems penguin chicks talk to each other
while still inside their shells.
Chicks in eggs sharing the same nest
cheep back and forth to each other.
Peepings help weak chicks catch up with strong ones,
and late chicks hatch out on time.

JANUARY
Attack

After ten, twelve, fifteen, or twenty hours of effort,
penguin chicks start rolling, chins first, out of splintered shells.
Parent penguins stand on nest rims, watching.
With beaks and feet, parent penguins push wet,
shivering chicks back into nests.
Nearly naked, wet from their eggs, feeble and blind,
chicks are quickly tucked under penguin bellies.
Hours pass before chicks stop shivering,
their down fluffed and dry.

Chips of broken shell cling to nest stones and curling seaweed.
Nests are slimy with egg remains.
Chunks of fractured shell crunch underfoot.
Chicks left frail and weak from the trial of hatching
lie like tiny, gray dust rags on the rocks.
These chicks, unmoving and unresponsive,
do not survive their first hours out of the egg.
Healthier, stronger chicks huddle like damp,
quivering pincushions sprouting beaks and feet.

Within minutes skuas on dark wings scan the rookery,
searching out dead and dying chicks.
Skua pairs rush at penguins guarding nests,
puffballs of chicks at their feet.
One skua forces the guardian penguin to dodge and duck
a four-foot wingspan, dangling talons, and gaping beak.
The other skua swoops in and takes the chick.
In a flash the chick is gone, dragged across the rocks,
killed instantly.

Terrified parent penguins, eye rings wide with alarm,
run in bumbling circles trying to find what is missing.
A chick already gone, already dead.
Skuas take weak chicks before strong ones.
Still, a third of the new chicks disappear
in the ravenous grasp of the skuas.

A chick's first egg-free hours are spent
drying and resting under a round, white penguin belly.
Soon the commotion and furor of hungry chicks
envelop the rookery in strident noise.
It is the babbling, screechy peeping of hundreds of hungry chicks.

Male penguins with nearly empty stomachs
are impatient to return to the sea.
Three days after hatching, females scatter into the rookery.
Fresh from the sea, with stomachs full, they
bring a good supply of food back to their chicks.
Shoving mates gently aside, females take over.
Fuzzy chicks, seven ounces each, as big as grapefruits,
sit wobbly and uncertain.

Leaning over chicks whose beaks are open wide, females
regurgitate partly digested krill out of their own crops
into the waiting throats of the chicks.
First meals splash on chick heads and bathe female
breast feathers in a soup that looks like blood
and cornmeal mixed together.
Krill stay a bright pink color
despite being swallowed by penguins.

With first feedings, chicks seem doomed
to drown in regurgitated food.
The rookery smells of it, the rocks are covered with it,
penguin parent breast feathers are streaked with it.
Parents and chicks learn quickly.
In a few days chicks thrust nodding heads and open beaks
directly down parent penguin throats.

Full Summer

In two weeks the chick's pearly gray down is filled out,
cottony and soft. A dark bill juts out between two beady black eyes.
Scaly, naked feet clutch nest stones — each foot has
three cigar-shaped toes, thick black toenails at the tips.
Penguin chicks resemble half-filled water balloons,
swelling and fattening with every feeding.

Antarctic days shine in full summer.
Slabs and blocks of glacier ice ride sea waves,
shimmering with reflected light. No storms threaten.
Light breezes sigh and murmur, carrying the rumble
and hubbub of penguin voices into a bright sky.

Summer days are as warm as thirty-five degrees.
The warmth is troublesome for penguins.
Feathers tight against fat bodies keep cold out
and keep heat in. Temperature control is difficult
for tiny chicks with undeveloped thermostats.
Parent penguins lift feather shafts and flippers,
letting heat escape and air circulate.
With heads up, beaks open, flippers stretched,
penguins cooling off look like sun worshipers.
Chicks keep cool by lying tummy down on nest stones,
necks extended and beaks open.
On warm days the rookery is quiet,
penguin voices are subdued and hushed.

Other chicks hatch out of eggs in other nests.
Fulmar chicks, with black, staring eyes and
prehistoric faces, are fuzzy and motionless under
their huge parents. Gull chicks, spindly and awkward, squat
on patches of moss, pelts of lichen, or directly on rocks.
Tern chicks, delicate and small, tuck into seaweedy
cracks in rocks, out of the sun,
and out of harm's way.

Blue-eyed shag parents skim over the waves,
catching fish for their chicks.
A shag chick has no down when it hatches.
In one week, tufts of skimpy brown down appear
on purplish skin, snippets of white
on eyebrows and head tops.
Shag chicks grow wing and tail quills
one month after hatching.

Sheathbills scrounge and scavenge rookeries.
Wandering inquisitive and unafraid, pigeon-sized sheathbills
annoy and distract parent birds, making them drop and discard food.
Scooping up the dropped food, sheathbills forage
for egg remains and even eggs.
A sheathbill nest with three or four chicks
is a messy assortment of feathers, bones, seaweed,
pebbles, and decayed food.

Late January — twenty-two days after hatching —
Adélie chicks are half the size of their parents.
Covered in sooty down, bottle-shaped chicks
seem dressed in oversized overcoats.
Able to run and waddle around, chicks stray from the nests.
Tugged, pushed, shoved, and pecked at, abused by neighboring
penguins, chicks often stray too far from home.
Many are taken by waiting skuas.

Half-grown chicks form nursery groups called crèches.
Gathering in squabbling huddles,
jabbering and whacking each other, chicks stay
together while their parents go to sea.

Returning parents feed only their own chicks.
Long, crowing calls announce returns.
Dashing out of the pack, chicks follow the
familiar sound of their own parents' voices.
The pandemonium of hundreds of squawking, crying
chicks explodes in the rookery.
Chicks running the wrong way, into the unwelcoming
flippers of another chick's parents,
are rudely pecked and driven off.

FEBRUARY · MARCH
First Molt

Six-week-old chicks start molting,
trading thick down for real penguin feathers.
Every spindly shank of down falls out, replaced by
perfectly formed adult feathers.
Skinnier than the parent penguins, the chicks
otherwise look the same.
Clouds of down blow into the air like puffs of smoke.
Winter's first chill winds blow the down away.

By late summer, molting penguin chicks look disarrayed.
Clumps of down still interrupt the smooth regularity
of grown-up penguin feathers. Chicks demand to be fed.
Sprinting around the rookery, chasing their parents,
calling in shrill, persistent voices, chicks stumble
and fall and get up again.

Chasing continues until the exasperated parents
turn and feed the chick, or race down the path,
plunging off the rocks, into the sea, to escape.
The chicks cannot eat enough.
Their appetites are out of control.
Winter survival depends on ample layers of fat
under fresh coats of adult penguin feathers.

APRIL
Winter Begins

The sun's light dims.
Lower in the sky, losing its warmth,
its bright flash dimming, the sun moves closer and closer
to the horizon. Little by little it sinks.
Dusky shadows creep across the sea, the shore, the island.

Ice spreads out from the land's edge.
The chicks, now properly and waggishly dressed
in Adélie penguin plumage, start
their first winter in cold Antarctic seas.
Perfect little Adélies, they leave the rookery
and make their way to the sea.
Nimble and spirited, able to dive and swim
on the first try, young penguins leap off rocks,
belly flop on waves, flashing white-feathered breasts.
Feeding on krill, diving for squid and fish,
the young penguins are independent and on their own.

Off the shore, swimming in dark circles near
the water's surface, leopard seals wait to
greet the new crop of Adélie penguins.
Some will be taken.
Most will escape and swim free.

Young penguins in the sea, feeding themselves,
leave adults to their yearly molt.
Old feathers, like old clothes,
wear out and have to be replaced.

Preparing for the ordeal of molting,
adult penguins fatten up, eating
until their weight is nearly doubled.
Like globes with flippers, penguins
totter up the stony shorelines of the
island, looking for safe places to wait out the molt.
Molting takes two or three weeks.
Penguins cannot swim while molting.

Adult penguin feathers form thick mats,
with feathers slightly curved and springy.
New feathers push old ones out.
Molting penguins look swollen.
An oil gland at the base of a penguin's tail
provides oil for preening, making feathers
greasy and waterproof.

By the end of April adult Adélies finish molting.
Leaving the breeding grounds, leaving the beaches,
penguins return to the sea.
A bounty of shed feathers remains behind,
scattered on all the beaches all around the island.

MAY
South Polar Winter Darkness

The sun's light is entirely gone.
Sea ice increases with every passing day.
Contours of sea and ice-covered land
are hidden in the darkness.

By midwinter Antarctic sea ice covers an area
nearly as large as the continent itself.
Forms of life needing little or no light
endure the dismal, inky blackness
of the under-ice world: diatoms, with fragile, lacy
bodies; protozoans; red and green algae;
tiny crustaceans like copepods and krill.
Coating delicate, crystalline ice surfaces,
a layer of living organisms grows so thick that
light would be blocked — if there were any.

Weddell seals, the only seals to spend winter
in Antarctica's seas, under the ice,
use a thousand-pound body and sharp teeth
to keep their breathing holes open.
Most Antarctic life — seals, whales, and birds —
migrate north when south polar winter darkness
comes down over land and sea.

What is it like under the ice?
What lives there? How does it live?
Penguins leave their rookeries, swim out to sea,
and disappear.
No one really knows where they go.
Perhaps they go to the very edge
where ice and water meet.

AUGUST
A New Year Begins

The months of darkness end
when the sun appears on the horizon.
The ruddy glow of the sun's first rays
streaks across Antarctic skies.
Adélie penguins begin their trek
across the sea ice, toward land.
Sea ice splinters and cracks.
Fissures and leads widen into ribbons of dark blue seawater.
Ice edges turn brownish-orange with phytoplankton blooms,
millions of tiny sea animals and plants burst into life.
Leopard seals prowl lanes of ice-free seawater.
Slabs and chunks of ice smash against each other,
snapping and clashing and yielding to the warming
of the sea and the air.
Around the island where the rookery is,

blocks of sea ice that held fast all winter
detach and float free.
Across a brightening sky
flights of migrating birds return
to their nesting colonies.

Out of the waves, sliding over ice floes,
tobogganing on white-feathered bellies,
hopping expertly from sea to rocks and ice,
Adélie penguins begin to appear.
Males first, scrabbling up the rocky slope,
enter the rookery with hoots and shouts.

Another Adélie penguin year begins.

GLOSSARY

Antarctica
The seventh continent, a land mass at the southern tip of the earth, the size of Europe and the United States together.

Adélie penguin
The best known of all penguins both popularly and scientifically; the "little man in evening dress," named by the French explorer and naval officer Jules Sébastien César Dumont d'Urville (1790–1842) in honor of his wife, Madame Adélie Dumont d'Urville.

Cloaca
An opening in birds through which eggs, droppings, and sperm all pass.

Copepod
A crustacean with four or five pairs of legs. Copepods feed on phytoplankton and are fed upon, in turn, by krill.

Crèches
Nursery groups formed by penguin chicks. Chicks huddle together for protection while their parents are away, feeding in the sea.

Diatoms
Microscopic, one-celled plants that usually live in colonies. Diatoms, in the form of algae, are a source of food for all kinds of marine life.

Floe
A mass of floating ice, usually eight to fourteen feet across or smaller, broken from a glacier, an ice shelf, or crumbling sea ice.

Fulmar chicks
The offspring of fulmars, which are large seabirds with broad wings. Males are bigger than females. Fulmars range over the sea, settling on coastal shores to breed.

Gentoo penguin
A kind of circumpolar Antarctic penguin, sometimes called "Johnny Penguin" or "Rockhopper." Thirty inches long, nine to thirteen pounds in weight, Gentoo penguins are the only penguins with white marks on the tops of their heads. They breed on Antarctic shores, lay two eggs, feed at sea, and leave the land for the sea in winter.

Glacier
A large mass of ice formed by compacted snow. A glacier's own weight forces it to move, to flow. Glaciers are frozen fresh water.

Guano
The droppings of seabirds.

Ice age
A period of time dominated by huge accumulations of ice over land.

Iceberg
A large, floating mass of ice, often rising to great height above the water. Icebergs break off of ice shelves and glaciers. Icebergs are frozen fresh water. The largest of them take years to melt away and disappear.

Krill
Crustaceans, or shrimplike animals, three inches long, found in great numbers in the

Southern Ocean. Krill are the base of the food chain in Antarctic seas, and are the primary food source for whales, seals, and many seabirds.

Leopard seal

A common seal of the Antarctic region. Slender, usually silver gray in color, leopard seals reach a length of five and a half feet. These seals feed on penguins, most often, and can be found wherever penguins gather. Leopard seals have many sharp teeth. Their pups are born in November, usually in the pack ice.

Meltwater

Running, seeping water produced when ice and snow melt.

Molting time

The time when a bird loses all of its old feathers and replaces them with new. Birds usually molt once a year.

Petrel

A large, diverse order of seabirds of ancient lineage, probably related to the penguins, although all petrels fly. Petrels have webbed feet, hooked bills, and tubular nostrils for filtering salt from their food. Petrels feed on plankton. All lay single eggs and take longer than most birds to raise their chicks. Many petrels live a long time — up to fifty years. The smallest ones, the storm petrels, patter over the water on webbed feet. Seeing them, early sailors were made to think of Saint Peter, and thus gave the petrels their name.

Phytoplankton

Floating, usually microscopic plant life living in marine water, and sometimes in fresh water. Phytoplankton forms the basis for all marine food webs. Phytoplankton is the primary producer of organic material in the sea.

Protozoans

Microscopic animals that are made up of a single cell, or group of identical cells, living in water.

Rookery

The colony, or breeding grounds, of seals, seabirds, and many other animals.

Sea ice

Ice that forms when seawater freezes, as distinct from glacier or iceberg ice, which is frozen fresh water.

Seawater lead

A channel of open water resulting when sea ice breaks apart.

Shag

A long-necked coastal bird with a thin, hooked bill and a long, stiff tail. In the Antarctic species shags have blue eyelids and patches of yellow on the upper part of the bill. Shags are black-backed with white breasts. They breed in colonies on cliffsides. On the sea they fly low over the water, using rapid wingbeats and short glides. They dive into the water to capture prey. To dry off after a dive they stand still, on land, with wings outstretched.

Sheathbill

A plump, all-white bird with gray feet and a brown bill. Sheathbills are about the size of pigeons. Females are smaller than males. Sheathbills eat anything — scavenging in rookeries for droppings, abandoned food, even eggs. They nest in solitary pairs, producing one to four chicks every season. Sheathbills live in the Antarctic region, migrating farther north in winter to South America and the Falkland Islands.

Skua

A gull-like predatory seabird with white flashes of feathers on primaries that show in flight. The skua's dark bill is hooked, its feet sharply clawed. Females are usually larger than males. Skuas nest in the Antarctic region, in solitary pairs, producing two chicks per season. They are fiercely protective of their young, attacking anything that comes near. Skuas fly strongly and quickly, pursuing their prey in a relentless, aggressive way. Skuas migrate to islands north of the Antarctic region in winter.

South Pole

One of two points on the earth's axis, at opposite ends of the earth, where magnetic forces are greatest. (The other is the North Pole.)

Southern Ocean

The region where the Atlantic, Indian, and Pacific oceans are contiguous. The Southern Ocean surrounds the continent of Antarctica.

Tern

A seabird with narrow, pointed wings, short legs, and webbed feet, smaller and slimmer than a gull. A tern will hover over its prey, flying gracefully and buoyantly with its sharp bill pointed downward. Terns exist all over the world. The Antarctic varieties nest in coastal zones, moving northward in winter. Terns produce one to three eggs and breed in colonies.

Weddell seal

A seal named for an early Antarctic explorer. The Weddell seals live farther south than any other seals. They feed on fish, give birth on the pack ice, and can reach a length of four feet. Weddell seals, in addition to being the southernmost seals, are also the deepest divers of any seals. They use echolocation — sounds echoing off ice — to find their way under the pack ice.